Hippopotamus

Hippopotamus

Facts About Hippopotamus A Colorful Picture Book For Kids

By: Flora Isaac

Flora Isaac

Copyright © 2016 by Flora Isaac

All rights reserved

No part of this book may be used or reproduced in any manner whatsoever without the express written permission of the publisher except for the use of brief quotations in a book review. Image Credits: Royalty free images reproduced under license from various stock image repositories. Under a creative commons licenses.

Hippopotamus

I am Bull, a male hippopotamus.

I stay with a "herd" or "pod" of young male hippos, some female hippos, and their babies.

Hippopotamus

I have a wife called Cow.

We have baby hippos called calves.

Female hippos give birth in the water.

We are the third biggest animals after the elephants and rhinoceroses.

Hippopotamus

We are also called "hippo" or "river horse."

We are found in Africa.

Hippopotamus

We like to place our bodies under the water during the day.

We stay in areas near swamps, rivers, and lakes.

Hippopotamus

We have eyes, ears, and a nose on top of our heads so we can breathe.

We can stay underwater for 5 minutes.

Hippopotamus

We have clear eyes that can see underwater.

Our nose and ears close quickly when we go deep underwater to avoid drowning.

We have a barrel-shaped body, a big mouth, and short legs.

We like to walk around after sunset until sunrise to eat.

Hippopotamus

We usually eat grass.

We can run faster than a human.

Hippopotamus

We are considered one of the most dangerous animals in the world.

We can live up to 45 years.

Hippopotamus

That is the life of a Hippopotamus. There are many other interesting animals out there. So, keep on reading and keep on learning about them.

We hope that you were able to see how wonderful and helpful these creatures are.

Made in the USA
Middletown, DE
02 September 2017